Germans
in Canada

Tina Schwartzenberger

Weigl

CALGARY

Published by Weigl Educational Publishers Limited
6325-10 Street SE
Calgary, Alberta
Canada T2H 2Z9
Web site: www.weigl.ca

All of the Internet URLs given in the book were valid at the time of publication. However, due to the
dynamic nature of the Internet, some addresses may have changed, or sites may have ceased to exist
since publication. While the author and publisher regret any inconvenience this may cause readers,
no responsibility for any such changes can be accepted by either the author or the publisher.

Library and Archives Canada Cataloguing in Publication

Schwartzenberger, Tina
        The Germans in Canada / Tina Schwartzenberger.

(Special Canadian communities)
Includes index.
ISBN 1-55388-129-X (bound).--ISBN 1-55388-131-1 (pbk.)

        1. German Canadians--Juvenile literature.
2. Germans--Canada--History--Juvenile literature.
I. Title. II. Series: Special Canadian communities
(Calgary, Alta.)

FC106.G3S39 2005   j971'.00431   C2004-907483-0

Printed and bound in China
1 2 3 4 5 6 7 8 9 0   09 08 07 06 05

Photograph Credits
Every reasonable effort has been made to trace ownership and to obtain permission to reprint
copyright material. The publishers would be pleased to have any errors or omissions brought
to their attention so that they may be corrected in subsequent printings.

Cover: The Kitchener-Waterloo Oktoberfest is the largest Bavarian festival in North America.

Cover: CP/Kitchener-Waterloo Record (David Bebee); **Jeff Brown:** pages 5, 12T, 17; **Canadian Pacific
Railway Archives:** page 7 (NS 8454); **Clipart.com:** pages 4T, 12B; **Corel Corporation:** pages 1, 15, 20;
Eyewire: pages 14T, 22R; **Glenbow Archives:** page 6 (nc-6-874); **Kitchener-Waterloo Oktoberfest:**
pages 8B, 9, 10, 14B, 18B; **Neue Welt:** page 19; **Photos.com:** pages 3T, 3MT, 3MB, 3B, 4B, 8T, 11, 13,
16T, 16B, 18T, 21L, 21R, 22L, 23L, 23M, 23R.

Project Coordinator Heather C. Hudak   **Design** Warren Clark   **Layout** Kathryn Livingstone
and Jeff Brown   **Copy Editor** Frances Purslow   **Photo Research** Kim Winiski   **Consultant**
Heidelberg Haus

We acknowledge the financial support of the Government of Canada through the Book Publishing
Industry Development Program (BPIDP) for our publishing activities.

Contents

Coming to Canada

When East Germany and West Germany became one country in 1990, the West German flag became a national symbol.

Germany is the seventh largest European country.

Germany is a country in central Europe. People born in Germany are called Germans. Over the past 300 years, many Germans have moved to Canada. Most of these German **immigrants** came to Canada in six large groups. The first settlers arrived before 1776. During the **American Revolution** between 1776 and the 1820s, many Germans came to Canada from the United States. From 1830 to 1880, another group moved to Ontario. More Germans moved to western Canada between 1874 and 1914. The final group arrived in Canada between World War I and World War II, and since 1945.

German Canadians practise the **culture** and **heritage** of their homeland. They learn the songs, language, celebrations, recipes, and legends of their **ancestors**. German Canadians have helped create the culture and communities of Canada today.

Germany

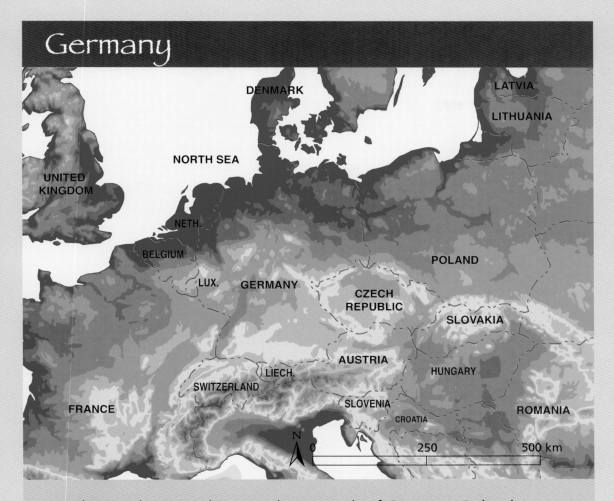

The North Sea and Denmark are north of Germany. Poland and the Czech Republic border Germany to the east. Austria is southeast of Germany. Switzerland is southwest of Germany. France, Belgium, and the Netherlands border Germany on the west.

Think About It

Can you find Germany on the map? What rivers, cities, and landmarks are nearby? What part of the world does your family come from? At the library, find a map of this country. Where is it located?

German Communities

Germans are the third-largest European cultural group in Canada. The British and the French are the only larger groups. German settlers came to Canada from eastern Europe, Russia, the United States, and Latin America. Until 1950, most of Canada's German-speaking settlers came from countries other than Germany. Since 1950, most German-speaking settlers have arrived from Germany.

Some people believe a man named Hans Bernard was the first German settler in Canada. Bernard bought land near Quebec in 1664. In 1750, 312 Germans came to Halifax. In 1753, about 1,450 Germans founded the town of Lunenburg in what is now Nova Scotia. By 1867, 200,000 Germans lived in Canada. Most lived in Ontario near the town of Berlin. Berlin was known as "Canada's German capital." Today, Berlin is called Kitchener.

The church was the focus of most German communities. Churches helped preserve the German language and culture.

Welcome to Canada

"Stepping out of the train station, in Toronto, on a brilliant sunny and warm day into a spotless, surprisingly quiet heart of the city made me feel optimistic and curious. It has been said that the first three people one meets in a strange place will shape one's opinion of that place forever.

WE'RE SAILING WEST. WE'RE SAILING WEST.
TO PRAIRIE LANDS SUNKISSED AND BLEST—
THE CROFTER'S TRAIL TO HAPPINESS.

About 152,000 German settlers lived in western Canada in 1911.

The first person was an English gentleman whom I asked for directions. He took the trouble of drawing a map for me and personally guiding me to the subway making sure that I was on my proper way.

The second person was an immigration officer who took one and a half-hours (without having had an appointment), making phone calls on my behalf. He was trying to line up job interviews with prospective employers and find a place for me to live.

The third person was my new landlady of the boarding house which the immigration officer had found for me. Not only did she make me feel warmly welcome but she also alerted some ex-tenants, who were Germans of my age, to the fact that a new compatriot had arrived. This assured me of a ready-made group of friends eager to introduce me to the mysteries and wonders of my new home. This was my first impression and special experience in Canada."

Think About It

Imagine it is the early 1900s. You have just arrived in Canada from Germany. Where would you live and work? Write a letter to family members in Germany. Tell them about your trip and life in Canada.

German-Canadian youth take part in festivals throughout the year.

Celebrating Culture

Germans brought their cultural **traditions** to Canada. These traditions include legends, songs, music, art, dance, food, and clothing. Many German traditions have religious meaning. These traditions are often part of holiday celebrations. The Christmas season is an important part of German culture. There are many German Christmas traditions.

German settlers in the 1700s brought their Christmas traditions to Canada. These settlers brought *tannenbaum*, or Christmas trees, **Advent calendars**, and gingerbread houses. Today, many Canadians from other cultures practise these traditions, too.

Oktoberfest

Oktoberfest is a well-known German celebration. Oktoberfest began when Crown Prince Ludwig of Bavaria, later King Ludwig I, wed Princess Therese von Sachsen-Hildburghausen in October of 1810. A horse race was part of the wedding celebration. The horse race took place every year after. In 1811, a farming fair was added to the horse race event. Booths serving food and drinks were added in 1818.

Today, the largest Oktoberfest celebration takes place in Munich, Germany. The festival lasts 2 weeks. It ends on the first Sunday in October. Many Canadian communities also celebrate Oktoberfest. These popular celebrations feature German food and drink. Some also host parades.

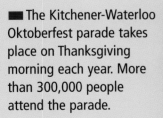

■ The Kitchener-Waterloo Oktoberfest parade takes place on Thanksgiving morning each year. More than 300,000 people attend the parade.

Think About It

What special holidays does your family celebrate? Think about these celebrations. Do any events or foods have special meaning?

Learning German Language

German is the official language of Germany. Many German Canadians speak German. German is an Indo-European language. It is much like the Netherlandic languages Dutch and Flemish. English is also an Indo-European language.

The German language has many **dialects**. Most dialects are either High German or Low German.

High German is spoken in the central and southern highlands of Germany, Austria, and Switzerland. It is the language used in the government, universities, books, and **media**. Low German is the spoken language of the lowlands in northern Germany. Low German is not often used in books or government.

More than 500,000 Canadians speak German.

Learning the Language

The German language is not difficult to learn. Try saying some of the following words and phrases.

English	German
Good morning	Guten Morgen
Goodbye	Auf Wiedersehen
Thank you	Danke schön
Please	Bitte
How are you?	Wie geht es Ihnen?
What time is it?	Wieviel Uhr ist es?
Good luck!	Viel Glück!

■ Many Canadian schools teach German language classes.

Think About It

Try practising these German language words. How do they compare to the English language? Do you speak any other languages? Try writing these words in your language.

Art and Culture

There are many traditional forms of German art. German Canadians often make this art to honour their heritage. For example, many German-Canadian women embroider. Embroidery is the art of decorating fabric with hand-sewn stitches.

German Canadians use many decorative **motifs** and designs in their craftsmanship. Hearts and tulips are the most popular. These appear on items such as grave markers, family albums, and furniture.

Fraktur is a style of writing that looks fractured, or broken. Fraktur comes from **medieval** writing. It makes drawings stand out on a page and words fade into the background. This tradition was brought from Switzerland to southern Germany.

Hand-embroidered towels hang as decorations over other towels or doors. Traditionally, this was a sign of a tidy home.

Germans often hand carve, paint, or embroider heart and tulip patterns on clothing, furniture, linens, and folk art.

Traditional Clothing

Traditionally, Germans wore clothes made from spun wool. People wore different kinds of clothing if they were married or single. Their clothing often showed what sort of job they worked, too. Many Germans still wear this clothing every day or for special occasions.

der Hut
hat

das Hemd
shirt

die Hosenträger
suspenders

die Lederhosen
leather pants

die Socken
socks

Think About It
What kinds of clothing do people from your culture and heritage wear? Do they wear it daily or only for special occasions?

Dancing Days and Musical Notes

An instrument similar to the accordion was invented in Berlin, Germany, in the 1820s.

Some German dances include the German Waltz, *Schuhplattler*, *The Landler*, *Das Muehlradl*, and *Watschentanz*.

Music and dance are important parts of German culture. There are many German dance and music groups in Canada. These groups perform at celebrations and festivals across the country. Traditional German folk dances are performed in Canada today. There are many types of dances. Couples perform most dances. Sometimes couples dance in large circles or in sets. There are also three-couple and four-couple dances. One German folk dance is called *Zwiefache*. During this dance, the performer moves very little. The best dancers can dance in a small area.

In the 1800s, a large number of Canadian musicians were German. During this time, German **composers** were some of the best in the world. Until 1860, Germans living in Quebec City, Montreal, Toronto, and Halifax were well known for their music.

In the late 1800s, many German musicians moved to Toronto. A. S. Vogt was a German Canadian. He founded the Toronto Mendelssohn **Choir**. More German singing groups began in Canada after 1950. Many German-Canadian clubs and community groups have choirs. In 1958, the German-Canadian Choir Association formed in Kitchener.

Germans sing special songs. Read the words of the song below.

O Tannenbaum

O Tannenbaum, o Tannenbaum,
wie treu sind deine Blätter!
Du grünst nicht nur zur Sommerszeit,
nein auch im Winter, wenn es schneit.
O Tannenbaum, o Tannenbaum,
wie treu sind deine Blätter!

■ In 1848, Queen Victoria's German husband, Prince Albert, decorated a Christmas tree at Windsor Castle. Soon, decorating a Christmas tree became a tradition in British, American, and Canadian homes.

O Christmas Tree

O Christmas tree, O Christmas tree!
How are thy leaves so **verdant**!
Not only in the summertime,
But even in winter is thy prime.
O Christmas tree, O Christmas tree,
How are thy leaves so verdant!

Think About It

Think about the songs you know. Are they the same as the German song? Try writing a song about early settlers, your community, or your heritage.

Hearty Fare

Germans brought many traditional recipes to Canada. They have been passed down to younger generations for hundreds of years. Germans cooked meals with foods they could find easily. It is easy to grow grain in Germany. Germans use grain to make many types of food. They bake more than 200 types of bread, for example. There is also plenty of **pasture** in Germany for cattle. As a result, Germans eat a great deal of butter, cheese, milk, and cream.

German food is very filling. Many people think of *sauerkraut* (cabbage) and *wurst* (sausage) when they think of German food. Two popular German desserts are *Schwartwälder Kirschtorte*, or Black Forest cake, and apple strudel. Northern Germans eat a great deal of meat and potatoes. Southern Germans eat fewer potatoes. Instead, they eat more grains. *Spätzle* is a common type of pasta noodle in southern Germany. German Canadians eat the traditional foods of their region in Germany.

Black Forest cake has many layers of chocolate cake, sour cherries, whipped cream, cherry liquor, and shaved chocolate curls.

German meals often have two to seven courses, including an appetizer, soup, main course, and after-meal treats called *Nachspeise*.

Lebkuchen (German Gingerbread)

Follow the recipe to make German gingerbread cookies.

Materials

37 millilitres golden syrup
120 mL butter
120 mL cup brown sugar
1 egg yolk
475 mL cups plain flour
5 mL tsp baking powder

15 mL ground ginger
2.5 mL cinnamon flour
currants, peel, cherries, and icing to decorate
large bowl
electric mixer
plastic wrap
rolling pin

gingerbread person cookie cutter
baking sheet
spatula

With an adult's help, use the electric mixer to beat the butter and sugar until they are creamy.

Beat in the egg yolk and syrup.

Slowly add the flour, baking powder, ginger, cinnamon.

Cover your hands with flour and knead the batter into dough.

Wrap the dough in plastic and place it in the fridge for 1 hour.

Brush flour on the rolling pin and the counter. Remove dough from the fridge. Roll the dough until it is about 1 centimetre thick. Use the cookie cutter to cut shapes from the dough.

Place each cookie about 2 cm apart on a greased baking sheet. Bake at 180 degrees Celsius for about 12 minutes.

Allow the cookies to cool. Remove them from the cookie sheet with a spatula.

Decorate each cookie with icing, peel, and cherries.

Think About It

Think about the foods your family eats during holiday meals. Do any of these foods belong to a certain culture? With an adult's help, try making a special family recipe.

Cultural Contributions

Germans have made many contributions to Canada since they began arriving in the 1600s. From farming to industry and museums to dance groups, German culture is an important part of the Canadian identity.

Germans helped settle Canada. German farmers used their farming skills in Canada. Germans from Russia were the first to grow what is now world-famous Canadian wheat on the Manitoba prairies. Germans helped make the Okanagan Valley in British Columbia western Canada's main fruit-growing area. Many Germans became well known for large harvests and for making new types of seed.

Churches, German clubs, and German immigrant parents created German Saturday School in 1900. German Saturday School teaches Canadian children of German heritage about their culture and traditions. Volunteer immigrant teachers give 2.5- to 3-hour lessons on Saturday mornings.

Before 1945, most Germans came to Canada in search of farmland.

Each year, a young woman is crowned Miss Oktoberfest in Kitchener-Waterloo.

In the News

Canada has many German-language newspapers. The first was *Halifax Neu-Schottländischer Calender*, created in 1788. The oldest German newspaper still in print in Canada is *Mennonitische Rundschau*. *Nordwesten*, a newspaper based in Winnipeg, Manitoba, began in 1889. The *Regina Courier* was first published in 1907. These two newspapers wrote stories for German Canadians of all religions. In 1970, these two papers joined. They became the *Kanada Kurier*.

Neue Welt is a German newspaper that began in southwestern Ontario in 2003.

Think About It

Think about your community. Are there any cultural centres and special groups? Which cultures do they represent? Do you belong to any special groups? Has any member of your family made a cultural contribution to Canada's heritage?

Further Research

How can I find more information about German culture?

- Libraries have many interesting books about German culture.

- The Internet offers some great Web sites dedicated to German culture.

Where can I find a Web site to learn more about German culture?

The Virtual Museum of Canada: Canada/German Migration
www.virtualmuseum.ca/Exhibitions/Migrations/english

Toronto Canadian-German Festival
www.germanfestival.ca

Germans in Alberta
http://collections.ic.gc.ca/albertans/people/german.html

Germans are the third oldest and third largest European cultural group in Canada. In 1996, 2,757,140 Canadians had German ancestry.

How can I find more Web sites about German culture?

Using a search engine, such as yahoo.ca or google.ca, type in different search terms. Some terms you might try include "Germans," "fraktur," and "wurst."

Make an Advent Calendar

Materials

green or red bath towel
felt
paper
thin, black felt-tip pen
fabric paint
cool-melt glue gun
ribbon
decorative braid
glitter glue
sequins
buttons
rope
small candy canes
stickers
scissors

1. Fold the bath towel in half. With the glue gun, glue the edges of the towel together. Leave 4 cm below the fold. This forms a pocket for the rope that hangs the calendar.

2. Glue the decorative braid around the edges of the towel to form a frame.

3. Draw the shape of a small Christmas stocking on paper. Cut out the shape.

4. Use the thin, black felt-tip pen to trace the stocking pattern on the felt. Repeat 25 times.

5. Cut out the felt stockings. Use the fabric paint to number each stocking from 1 to 25.

6. Glue the bottom and sides of each stocking. Do not glue the front or top of the stockings.

7. Place the stockings on the towel.

8. Decorate the stockings with ribbon, glitter glue, sequins, or buttons. Be careful not to cover up the number.

9. Place the rope through the pocket at the top of the towel. Put one candy cane or sticker into each stocking pocket. Hang your new Advent calendar on the wall.

Think About It

Advent calendars are an important part of German culture. Search the Internet to find other important symbols. What are some important symbols in your culture?

What Have You Learned?

1	2	3	4	5
Where is Germany?	When did Germans first arrive in Canada?	Where did many Germans settle?	What are the two types of German language?	What Christmas traditions did Germans bring to Canada?

6
Name two German art forms.

7
What is the name of a well-known German dance?

8
What foods do Germans traditionally eat?

9
What is the oldest German newspaper in Canada?

10
Name two contributions Germans made to Canada.

Glossary

Advent calendars calendars with a gift for each day in the month before Christmas

American Revolution a time between 1763 and 1820s, when American colonies fought for freedom from Great Britain's rule

ancestors people from the past who are related to modern people

choir people who sing together as a group

composers people who write music

culture the customs, traditions, and values of a nation or people

dialects different forms of a language

heritage traditions passed down to younger generations

immigrants people who come to a country to live and work

media newspapers, magazines, radio, and television

medieval having to do with a time between 500 and 1450 known as the Middle Ages

motifs single or repeated designs or colours

pasture grass-covered land used for grazing livestock

traditions cultural rituals, customs, and practices

verdant lush and green

Index